THE END OF
Christendom
AND THE FUTURE OF
Christianity

Christian Mission and Modern Culture

EDITED BY
ALAN NEELY, H. WAYNE PIPKIN,
AND WILBERT R. SHENK

In the series:

Believing in the Future, by David J. Bosch

Write the Vision, by Wilbert R. Shenk

Truth and Authority in Modernity,
by Lesslie Newbigin

Religion and the Variety of Culture,
by Lamin Sanneh

The Mission of Theology and Theology as Mission,
by J. Andrew Kirk

The End of Christendom and the Future of Christianity,
by Douglas John Hall

THE END OF

Christendom

AND THE FUTURE OF

Christianity

———

DOUGLAS JOHN HALL

TRINITY PRESS INTERNATIONAL
Harrisburg, Pennsylvania

Gracewing.

First U.S. edition
published 1995 by
TRINITY PRESS INTERNATIONAL
P.O. Box 1321
Harrisburg, PA 17105
U.S.A.

First British edition
published 1995 by
GRACEWING
2 Southern Avenue
Leominster
Herefordshire HR6 0QF
England

Trinity Press International is a division of The Morehouse Group.

Trinity Press International is a division of
the Morehouse Publishing Group.

Copyright © 1997 Douglas John Hall

Cover design: Brian Preuss

Library of Congress Cataloging-in-Publication Data

Hall, Douglas John, 1928–
    The end of Christendom and the future of Christianity / Douglas
  John Hall.
        p.   cm. – (Christian mission and modern culture)
    Includes bibliographical references.
    ISBN 1-56338-193-1 (pbk. : alk. paper)
    1. Christianity – 20th century. 2. Church and the world.
  I. Title. II. Series.
  BR121.2.H315   1997
  270.8'29–dc21   96-49944
                                                              CIP

Gracewing ISBN 0 85244 421 4

Printed in the United States of America

98   99   00   01   6   5   4   3   2

Contents

Preface to the Series

Both Christian mission and modern culture, widely regarded as antagonists, are in crisis. The emergence of the modern mission movement in the early nineteenth century cannot be understood apart from the rise of technocratic society. Now, at the end of the twentieth century, both modern culture and Christian mission face an uncertain future.

One of the developments integral to modernity was the way the role of religion in culture was redefined. Whereas religion had played an authoritative role in the culture of Christendom, modern culture was highly critical of religion and increasingly secular in its assumptions. A sustained effort was made to banish religion to the backwaters of modern culture.

The decade of the 1980s witnessed further momentous developments on the geopolitical front with the collapse of communism. In the aftermath of the breakup of the system of power blocs that dominated international relations for a generation, it is clear that religion has survived even if its institutionalization has undergone deep change and its future forms are unclear. Secularism continues to oppose religion, while technology has emerged as a major source of power and authority in modern culture. Both confront Christian faith with fundamental questions.

The purpose of this series is to probe these developments

from a variety of angles with a view to helping the church understand its missional responsibility to a culture in crisis. One important resource is the church's experience of two centuries of cross-cultural mission that has reshaped the church into a global Christian *ecumene*. The focus of our inquiry will be the church in modern culture. The series (1) examines modern/postmodern culture from a missional point of view; (2) develops the theological agenda that the church in modern culture must address in order to recover its own integrity; and (3) tests fresh conceptualizations of the nature and mission of the church as it engages modern culture. In other words, these volumes are intended to be a forum where conventional assumptions can be challenged and alternative formulations explored.

This series is a project authorized by the Institute of Mennonite Studies, research agency of the Associated Mennonite Biblical Seminary, and supported by a generous grant from the Pew Charitable Trusts.

Editorial Committee

ALAN NEELY
H. WAYNE PIPKIN
WILBERT R. SHENK

Foreword

The title of this book is intended to suggest the overall hypothesis that I want to develop in it. Briefly put, it is my belief that the Christian movement can have a very significant future — a responsible future that will be both faithful to the original vision of this movement and of immense service to our beleaguered world. But to have *that* future, we Christians must stop trying to have the kind of future that nearly sixteen centuries of official Christianity in the Western world have conditioned us to covet. That coveted future is what I mean when I use the term "Christendom" — which means literally the dominion or sovereignty of the Christian religion. Today Christendom, so understood, is in its death throes, and the question we all have to ask ourselves is whether we can get over regarding this as a catastrophe and begin to experience it as a doorway — albeit a narrow one — into a future that is more in keeping with what our Lord first had in mind when he called disciples to accompany him on his mission to redeem the world through love, not power.

I will develop this thesis over the course of four chapters, whose titles designate the stages of my argument. These chapters were first developed for the Hayward Lectures of Acadia University in Wolfville, Nova Scotia, and later for the Theological Lectureship of the Associated Mennonite Seminaries in Elkhart, Indiana. The fourth chapter was developed in a slightly altered form for the Theology and Worship Committee of the Presbyterian Church (U.S.A.) and was privately circulated as its "Occasional Paper No. 5" under the title *An Awkward Church*.

1

The Decline and Fall of Christendom

Great Expectations —
and Ecclesiastical "Future Shock"

To say that Christianity in the world at large is undergoing a major transition is to indulge in understatement. What is happening is nothing less than the winding down of a process that was inaugurated in the fourth century of the common era. To the great shift that began to occur in the character of the Christian movement under the Roman emperors Constantine and Theodosius I, there now corresponds a shift of reverse proportions. What was born in that distant century, namely, the imperial church, now comes to an end. That beginning and this ending are the two great social transitions in the course of Christianity in the world. All the alterations in between them (and of course history *is* change) are minor ones by comparison.

To confess faith in Jesus Christ at this time is therefore to do so within the context of a religion whose historical destiny is undergoing a metamorphosis — literally, a change of form or shape (*morphē*). This religion has been a great power in the world. It can still be regarded here and there as though its imperial status were yet intact, but it is nevertheless in the process of being reduced. Although some semblance of Christendom may find a new home in Africa, Asia, and Latin America, its period of Western dominance is over.

Attempts to confess the faith that are not cognizant of this situation, and especially those that deliberately ignore the changed circumstances of the church in the world, cannot succeed as authentic confessions of the faith, for they avoid or fail to grasp the status of the confessing body itself, which is now no longer one of singular power and influence but that of a peripheral voice. Precisely as such, however, this voice may also be a prophetic one. From the edges of imperial societies, a disciple community possessing awareness of its changed relation to power can exercise a prophetic vigilance for God's beloved world that, as part of the world's power-elite, it never did and never could achieve.

What is lacking in nearly all of the formerly prominent Christian bodies of the West is just this awareness and acceptance of their changed relation to power. Rather, they cling to their accustomed modus operandi, their imagined status vis-à-vis the powerful, and in doing so they forfeit the opportunities for truth telling and justice that historical providence is affording them. Thus, too many attempts at faith's confession simply do not "come off" because they still assume a Constantinian framework. They speak as though from positions within the power centers of society. They presuppose a certain right to assume the stand that they promulgate. Therefore they almost always fail to convince anyone outside the fold or even to raise significant questions. Usually they do not develop a sufficient rationale for their claims — sufficient either theologically or apologetically. Because they presume upon the supposed authority of the church, these confessional "stands" usually neither sway those who for sentimental or other reasons remain within the churches nor touch the consciences of those outside the churches. Presumption upon the past power and glory of Christendom is perhaps the greatest deterrent to faith's real confession in our present historical context.

The decline and humiliation of Christendom in the West is, I have said, a process. It is not a matter of sudden death. Indeed, in those places where Christianity has seemed to be extinguished, there has often been an interesting kind of resuscitation. The experience of the churches behind the so-called iron curtain of the immediate past is the prime example of this. Christianity in the Marxist-Leninist lands did not die so much as it found itself being put to death. There could be no place for this "opiate" in the new society! But precisely the abruptness of this alteration in status, combined with the fact that it was imposed by a hostile and unpopular ideology, caused many, who like their counterparts in the West would certainly have been ready to wend their way into the religion-less world, to pause. The suppression of the faith was in many ways the reason for its resurgence as a lively and critical posture. For significant numbers of people in these countries, Christianity represented the spiritually and intellectually liberating alternative to a very oppressive and life-draining system, a world lacking not only truth and transcendence but also, conspicuously, beauty. It has been said that "the blood of the martyrs is the seed of the church," and something like that was again demonstrated in the history of Christianity in European communist lands following World War II. Where "the end of the Constantinian era" (Günther Jacob) was swift, obvious, and forced, it evoked a state of resistance that prompted an imaginative reassessment of the faith. It will be interesting to observe the fate of Christianity in those same contexts, now that the official threat to the church's existence has been removed.

The "normal" process of Christendom's decline is, by contrast, very gradual. In some places, including much of our own continent, it can even appear that Christendom is alive and well, unless one looks beneath the surface. In such contexts, Christian congregations and even whole denominations are able to carry on as usual, as if nothing had happened. But this response is often visibly contrived, and it is viable only as long as the economic conditions of churches are relatively sound. With each new decade, more and more Christians are driven to realize the watershed through which Christendom is passing.

All the same, the transition to the post-Constantinian, or post-Christendom, situation is hardly a new phenomenon. Though unnoticed by many, the dissolution of Christendom has already been in process for a century or two. It would be impossible to read the philosophic and literary works of the Western world from the eighteenth century onward without realizing that new attitudes were in the making which, if they did not topple the Christian establishment immediately and dramatically (as was attempted in revolutionary France), would certainly do so eventually. Whereas eighteenth-century rationalism was ameliorated by evangelical pietism — and nineteenth-century "pagan" romanticism by the Christian romanticism of Schleiermacher, the Oxford Movement, and other groups — the process of secularization was well under way, and, despite religious revivals of various types, it has continued to be so.

If one reflects upon the other end of the Christendom phenomenon, its beginning, one is not surprised that it should be slow in ending. The inauguration of Christendom occurred in the fourth-century C.E.; this is simply a fact of history. But even dictatorial governments do not inaugurate such complex phenomena as religion. Rome could no more initiate Christianity than Moscow could dissolve it. After the codes of Theodosius and Justinian, paganism still flourished in many places, especially in the countryside. In fact, the term "pagan" derives from the Latin *paganus,* meaning villager or rustic — roughly the equivalent of "yokel." These country folk were not quick to change their allegiances from the old gods to the new religion ordered up by Rome. Besides, the tribes of the north, some of which dealt Rome itself its fatal blow, were not fully christianized for centuries. Moreover, even at its height and despite its often violent efforts, Christianity never managed to rid Europe of alternative faiths — notably Judaism and Islam.

We should not suppose, therefore, that the *terminus ad quem* (the other end) of this same religious process would be anything but gradual. People do not alter their systems of belief overnight. The vestiges of Christendom are still very much present even in the most secularized populations of the formerly "Christian" West, and they will never wholly vanish.

But this does not mean that the points of transition at both ends of this phenomenon are so gradual and inconspicuous as to be less than great transitions. Clearly, something happened to the Christian movement when it was adopted by the Roman imperium in the fourth century, and something is now happening to it as it gives way to new cultural realities, including widespread secularism and religious pluralism. The ending of Christendom is not as obvious to us as its beginning, partly because we are involved directly in its ending. But that it is occurring can be doubted only by those who do so on the basis of ignorance, disinterest, or because of vested interests in the preservation of the imperial model of the church.

Understandably enough, there are vested interests in the retention of Christendom, and they are potent ones. After all, a phenomenon existing for fifteen or sixteen centuries is very well established indeed! Its establishment, as we will observe more fully presently, is by no means only a legal affair — though even in situations (like our own) where the church was never established in the formal or *de jure* sense, there are legal dimensions that resist change (such as, in North America, the limiting of taxation on church properties). More entrenched are the cultural dimensions of establishment. Everywhere in the West and in those parts of the East that have been dominantly Christian, the Christian religion has permeated culture. It has influenced every aspect of public life, of art and literature and music, of folk wisdom, of personal relationships, of pageantry, and so forth. Even those who have long since ceased to have anything to do with the churches may be heard to express sentiments, values, biases, and also (alas!) prejudices that have their origin in Christendom.

When I speak of vested interests in sustaining the imperial model of the church, however, I have especially in mind ties of a more internal and institutional character. Though the Christian faith entered the world as a movement containing provocative anti-institutional elements, it eventually expressed itself in well-defined institutional forms. Such forms, as we know from history, regularly outlast the visions and objectives that give rise to them. Just as the ecclesiastical structures and offices produced by the faith and doctrine of the Middle Ages endured long after the effective end of that age (the mid-fifteenth century), so the institutions of Christendom survive today, and they will in all likelihood continue, in various permutations, to survive for centuries. The effective "end of the Constantinian era" does not mean the simultaneous end of ecclesiastical and paraecclesiastical structures. Indeed, in some cases ecclesiastical structures may well become more prominent with the waning of the institution precisely because they are under duress. The papacy was never so vociferous and ostentatious as it was following the demise of the medieval "Age of Belief." We have witnessed enough in our own lifetime to understand that the structures of Christian denominations, like the bureaucracies of governments and corporations, will defend their existence as long as possible.

I believe that commitment to the established institutional model of the church — to Christendom in its various institutional forms — is the single most important cause of inertia and the retardation of intentional and creative response to this great transition. Yet even those of us who find the entrenchment of Constantinianism an impediment and who are often literally sickened by the resultant falseness and inertness of the churches are ourselves, most of us, in one degree or another still dependent upon the continuation of Christendom. Even if our livelihood does not depend upon the maintenance of the old ecclesiastical forms, few of us are either spiritually or materially equipped for the kind of nonestablished situation that pertained in the early church or for the disestablishment that has been the fate of significant numbers of serious Christians throughout the history of Christendom and is found in many contexts also today. The vested interests that keep Christendom from disappearing even when it is clearly a drawback to the emergence of a livelier form of the church do not, all of them, belong to popes, ecclesiastical bureaucrats, and other powerful segments in the contemporary churches. They are to be found in almost all of us. One suspects that much of our ecclesiology and church polity is informed by a process of corporate rationalization aimed at justifying the status quo.

The effective end of Christendom is, after all, a traumatic historical experience — a future shock far greater, in fact, than the demise of classes, nations, or empires. Not only has Christendom outlived the Roman, the Holy Roman, the British, the Russian, and other empires that espoused it; not only has it survived the many systems with which it has been identified (the imperial, the feudal, the early mercantile, etc.); not only has it lasted well beyond the dysfunctioning of monarchies, aristocracies, and other seemingly permanent institutions of the West, but the trauma produced by Christendom's demise is qualitatively different from any of these other endings. It has to do with the type of expectancy surrounding Christendom and is therefore rightly named "future shock."

That expectancy was of another order. Although it had very definite mundane dimensions and consequences, it was at base supramundane in nature. The church, it was felt, would be the doorway — the *only* doorway, most Christians believed — to eternity. Thus it would not only endure (had not the Lord himself assured his disciples that the very "gates of hell" would not "prevail" against it?), but it would prosper! Other institutions — kingdoms, political systems, governments — might come and go; even divinely ordained offices and social structures could pass away, their usefulness ended; but as the portal of God's own kingdom, the church could expect a glorious future.

The shock created by the prospect of Christendom's ending is engendered in particular by this kind of expectation. The future that must be contemplated now seems altogether to contradict the future that centuries of official Christianity taught Christians to anticipate. Christian mission, under the conditions of imperial Christianity in the West, has been confused with Christian expansionism. We tend to equate the great ages of missionary activity with those moments in history, particularly in the nineteenth century, in which the Christian religion gained more quantitative power in the world, and more territory. Such an equation certainly ought to be questioned if one takes the New Testament as one's guide. But that confusion of Christian mission with Christendom's victories was a natural confusion, given the whole mythos of historical growth that has seemed to almost every Christian to be built into the faith itself.

In order to appreciate better the incongruity between Christendom's conventional expectations and the reduced destiny that now seems to open out to us, we will consider two expressions of typical Christendom scenarios that come to us from sources close enough to our period to remind us how very recently Christians entertained a conception of the Christian future markedly different from the evidence that now invades Christian consciousness.

How We Have Viewed Ourselves

Søren Kierkegaard wrote his famous *Attack Upon Christendom* in the middle of the nineteenth century, but the image of Christendom depicted in that collection of self-financed pamphlets is by no means typical of the way Christians have seen themselves and their religious enterprise. Even after Kierkegaard's work became known outside Denmark — which did not happen until the second or third decade of the present century — his *Attack* seemed to most Christians strange, perhaps even mad. The typical self-image contained in most theological and ecclesiastical literature well into the present century (and it is still prominent in many ecclesiastical circles) could only make Kierkegaard's castigation of official Christianity appear exaggerated and offensive.

Almost any popular work on the subject prior to the end of

World War II would serve to illustrate the self-image to which I refer. The two that I will explore briefly have been chosen because the first gives us a sampling of the way Christians (particularly Christians of the mainstream, liberal denominations) have understood their past history, and the second is an extrapolation of this same self-understanding for the purpose of envisioning the Christian future.

In 1934, a collection of essays was published under the title *The Christian Message for Today* (Jones et al.: 1934). Its subtitle describes the book as "A Joint Statement of the World-Wide Mission of the Christian Church," and its authors were some of the great American Protestants of the period. Although many aspects of this book warrant our study today, what strikes one with particular force is its way of "reading" the Christian past. The object of the authors, as the title and subtitle suggest, is to offer an inspiring call to Christian mission "today." However, celebration of the Christian present and future requires a foundational history that can also be celebrated, and this is just what we are given.

> From its inception Christianity has been expanding geographically. Beginning as an inconspicuous Jewish sect, one of the least of the many cults seeking to make a place for themselves in the Greco-Roman world, it early outgrew its Jewish swaddling clothes, became cosmopolitan in membership, and within less than four centuries was the dominant faith of the Roman Empire (:149).

Already in this little summary of Christian beginnings we note two interesting and well-rehearsed themes that frequently appear in this type of literature: (1) the humble origins of the faith in a Jewish context that was obviously too narrow for it —

a theme with only slightly cloaked marcionitic and possibly anti-Jewish overtones; and (2) the assumption that Christianity's adoption by Rome was a fortuitous, indeed perhaps a divinely ordained, eventuality. Yet, as the historical outline continues, we learn that the Christian religion was also too expansive for Rome, which could serve only as a temporary vehicle for its promotion.

> When the Roman Empire collapsed, Christianity, although by that time closely associated with it, not only survived but won to its fold the barbarians who were the immediate cause of the overthrow, spread into regions in Northern and Western Europe which had not before known it, and became the chief vehicle for the transfer of the culture of the ancient world to the Europe of medieval and modern times (ibid.).

Here is another familiar theme of the story Christians learned to tell of themselves: Christianity is the bearer of the highest culture, preserving what is true, good, and beautiful from the past yet transcending the political forms that manifested these values and virtues. The same theme persists in the next statement of the thumbnail sketch of Christian progress.

> In the middle ages Christianity was an integral part of the intellectual, social, economic and political patterns of the day. Its theology was formulated in terms of the prevailing scholasticism and it was apparently a bulwark of the existing feudal society.
>
> Yet when the medieval world disappeared, Christianity persisted. Not only so, but when, in the Fifteenth and Sixteenth Centuries, European peoples spread into the Americas and won footholds in Asia, Christianity

went with them, became the faith of the peoples whom the Europeans conquered, and ameliorated the cruelties of the conquest (:149–50).

To be sure, this is a nuanced statement. It is not blatantly racist or imperialistic. Christianity as such is not identified with the conquerors, and it is (rightly) claimed that the faith "ameliorated the cruelties of the conquest." But if this episode in Christian history were summarized in two paragraphs today, their content would be very different. From the perspective of present assumptions at work in liberal and moderate churches, it would be hard to avoid the hint of both racism and imperialism even in this rather careful summation.

The statement now moves toward articulation of the underlying historical-theological hypothesis informing it — the continuous ascendancy of Christianity, setbacks notwithstanding.

Occasionally Christianity has suffered major territorial reverses. In the Seventh and Eighth Centuries Islam won from it vast areas and numerous peoples. In the Fourteenth and Fifteenth Centuries the wide-flung posts of Nestorian Christianity in Asia were almost wiped out by Tamerlane and his cohorts. In the present century the church in Russia has been dealt staggering blows. Yet in spite of the fact that Christianity has never fully regained the ground from which it was driven in these defeats, usually it has more than made good in other regions the area lost. Never has it been so widespread as today (:150).

What surely strikes the contemporary reader of this paragraph most forcibly is the almost innocent manner in which both Christian failure and success are interpreted in straightforwardly territorial terms. Not only is it assumed that (as noted earlier) mission means expansion, but the expansion in question means the acquisition of more territory. When I employ the term "imperial church" to the model dating from Constantine, it is this conception of the church that I have in mind. Generously, one may say that Christian imperialism is gentler, usually, than that of worldly empires; the Christian "conquers for Christ," at least in intention. But what the Christian so motivated wants "for Christ" seems in the end not essentially different from what worldly empires want — more territory. This is why it is not quite sufficient to think of the Constantinian church only numerically in terms of numbers of people ("the church as majority," as I sometimes phrase it). This mentality also usually extends to the control of space as well as what the space contains by way of population and culture.

The author now presses home his conclusion — the point to which his historical summary has been moving all along.

In the history of mankind no other religion has been professed over so large a proportion of the globe or by so many people. From the outset Christianity has claimed for its message universality: it has maintained that it has a gospel for all men. More nearly than any other faith it has progressed toward the attainment of that goal. While of the other two great surviving missionary religions, one, Buddhism, has long been practically stationary, and the other, Islam, has made few if any major gains in the past hundred years, Christianity, in spite of the many obstacles which beset its path, is still spreading. In no similar length of time have its boundaries expanded so rapidly and so widely as in the past century and a half (:150–51).

I will refrain from commenting on the obviously anachronistic assumptions about "the other two great surviving missionary religions" and the even more anachronistic conclusions concerning the magnificent expansion of the Christian religion. What should capture our attention here, beyond what has been said earlier, is the way in which this kind of analysis (and this is only one instance of an entire genre) automatically leads to the assumption not only that Christianity is going to enjoy a still greater future but that it and it alone deserves such a destiny, for it is superior to any other. Its qualitative superiority is demonstrated by its quantitative success, and its quantitative success is because of its qualitative superiority.

The second document we will consider applies the same thinking to the Christian future. In the final pages of a work, published in 1926, bearing the currently intriguing title *The Dominion of Man,* E. Griffith-Jones asks about "the place and function of the Church in the regenerated social order" (Griffith-Jones 1926:311).[1] Not surprisingly, his answer begins with an allusion to the "Great Commission":

> The first mandate [the Church] received from its Risen Master was to go forth into all the world and to preach the Gospel to every creature. This mandate is still in force, for the work has not been accomplished; after two thousand years there are uncounted millions of the human race who have never heard the Christian message. *We are, however, envisaging a time when this will have been effectively done, and when the whole race has long been under the sway of the Gospel* (ibid., emphasis added).

Contemporary readers may well be astonished at this statement, but they are reminded that a journal still flourishes that bears the name that it does because prominent elements in all the major denominations of this continent fervently believed, not long ago, that the twentieth century would be *The Christian Century!* Griffith-Jones, having endorsed that same credo, proceeds to outline the church's role in the fully christianized society of the near future.

> Then the Church will be able to give herself to a still higher task. It will be hers to evangelize each fresh generation before the forces of evil have had their chance of poisoning the virgin soul of the new humanity, of training it in the knowledge and nurture of the Lord from the beginning, and of developing its spiritual nature into fullness and power. It will once more join its forces with science, and with literature, and with art, and be their inspiration in every effort to enlighten, and enrich and beautify life. It will hallow the relation of Man to Nature, and sanctify all the uses to which his ever-enlarging control of her energies will be put. It will safeguard social privileges from abuse, and political power from tyranny. It will spiritualize commerce and trade and industry, and humanise the relations of those who co-operate in the production of wealth, or take part in its distribution in the exchanges and markets of the world. The distinction between the secular and the sacred will disappear from human life, for all that is secular will be sanctified. When this ideal state will be realised, the world will once more be God's world, and His "will be done on earth as it is done in Heaven" (:311–12).

The author pauses. "Is this a fanciful picture?" he asks (perhaps in the interim having looked up from his desk into the streets below!). On the contrary, he answers:

It is but a faint sketch of a world which has been in the making since the light first broke over the primeval chaos, and the earth was prepared for man's coming, that he might take his place as God's vice-regent and fellow in bringing such a world into being. This is the "final end" of the Providential Order, "the last," for which the first was made. All that remains to be done in order that it may be realized, is that Man should at last rise to the fulfillment of his Providential function, and join his energies with the mighty power and wisdom of God, in loving obedience and joyful service.

On the sunlit hills of time — the City of God, the Commonwealth of the Redeemed! (:312).

The liberal version of the Christian future, of which this is a sterling instance, seems in some ways even more triumphalistic than "orthodox" Christian futurology; for the other-worldliness of the latter was translated by the liberals into this-worldly forms of realization, thereby rendering them quite visibly utopian. Like so many thinkers of his epoch, Griffith-Jones was caught up in the euphoria of great expectations that gripped the souls of privileged persons in the nineteenth and early twentieth centuries. His vision of the future both of the world and of the church was an extension of his liberal ideology of progress. Reading the rest of his book, one realizes that he was by no means unaware of human problems; in fact, the bracketed subtitle of the book is "Some Problems in Human Providence." The problems, however, come nowhere near the dogma of original sin. The overruling passion of the author's mind was a worldview so utterly optimistic that the negations he entertained were soon swept away by the full tide of his positive thinking.

And we are speaking of 1926! Only eight years earlier, Europe had witnessed the problematic and tragically inconclusive end of the bloodiest war in human history. Within three years the stock markets of the world would crash, and already millions of poor people were living seismographs of the coming Great Depression. Moreover, in 1926 it was possible for Christians to interpret both the world and their own place in it very differently from Griffith-Jones. Karl Barth in Europe and Reinhold Niebuhr in Henry Ford's Detroit were commenting upon the works of God and Western humanity, as well as the empirical church, in terms 180 degrees removed from Griffith-Jones's happy outlook.

Although Griffith-Jones paints his picture of the Christian future in liberal terms, it is nevertheless a version of a very old conception of the character and prospects of Christendom. Different ages of Christian history have assigned this conception of the church differing details, but the broad themes persist. They include such ideas as that it is the Christian mandate to turn the whole world, if possible, into church; that this mandate comes from Jesus himself; that other religious faiths are not to be honored seriously but are to be seen, at best, as preliminary stages on the way to truth; that humanity is separate from the rest of nature, intended by God to dominate the natural order and enabled by Christ to do so, and so on.

This scenario is precisely what can no longer be sustained. Today, informed and reflective Christian thinkers would have to describe the emergent future of the Christian faith in ways that diverge markedly from those assumed in both of these relatively recent studies. It is a very different scenario that is gleaned from Langdon Gilkey's *Through the Tempest* (1991), or Hans Küng's *Theology for the Third Millennium* (1988), or

David Tracy's *Plurality and Ambiguity* (1987). Both *The Oxford Illustrated History of Christianity* (McManners:1990) and
Christianity: A Social and Cultural History (Kee:1991), two
of the most ambitious recent surveys of Christianity, tell the
Christian story, past, present, and future, in a manner that
would have seemed utterly foreign to Griffith-Jones and the
authors of *The Christian Message for Today*.

Many influences have brought about this historiographic
change: the decline of Christianity in the West; the decline of
the West itself; the failure of the modern vision; the new consciousness of their own worth on the part of non-European
peoples; a critical perception of the technological society on
the part of many who have experienced its most advanced
forms; the impact of religious and cultural pluralism, especially perhaps in North America; and (not least of all) the
self-criticism of serious Christianity, its recognition of its own
questionable triumphalism, of patriarchalism, of the equation
of the Christian mission with Euro-American imperialism,
and so forth. "To a great extent," writes the Dutch theologian
Hendrikus Berkhof, expressing a new realism about Christian
history that is shared by many reflective Christians in our time,
"official church history is the story of the *defeats* of the [Holy]
Spirit" (1979:422).

With that quite radical summation by a theologian who is
far from radical, I will bring this first chapter to a close. I
have argued that Christendom, and the kind of future that
Christendom conditioned us all to expect, has been decisively
called into question. The next stage in my argument will be
to ask, "What are the typical responses of Christians today — especially in North America — to the 'altered status'
of Christianity in our fast-changing planet?"

2

Ecclesiastical Responses to the End of the Constantinian Era

As I pointed out at the beginning of this volume, the thesis I am developing is that the Christendom phase of the Christian movement is drawing to a decisive close. It has constituted a very long period in Western history, lasting from the fourth century of the common era right into our own time; but now we recognize — or we ought to — that it was a phase, and neither the permanent nor the only possible way of being the church. Therefore we have to ask ourselves: Insofar as we are serious about this faith, what kind of model or conception of the Christian movement ought to replace the imperial, or Constantinian, or majority model — what we call "Christendom"? I believe that the future the Christian movement can have is a significant one, but we will be able to claim it only if we give up trying to cling to the Christendom model. Such is my basic thesis.

At the end of the last chapter, I reminded you that many theologians and faithful Christians all over the world have been and are trying to come to terms with all this. Many, like Hans Küng, Karl Rahner, Karl Barth, Jacques Ellul, Jürgen Moltmann, Rosemary Ruether, Dorothee Sölle, Gustavo Gutiérrez, and others have put forward analyses of the past and visions for the future to which attention ought to be paid throughout the churches. Such thinkers have adopted a new kind of realism about the Christian past and a new kind of hope (not to be confused with optimism) about the Christian future.

On the whole, however, neither this realism nor this hope has informed, consistently, the thinking and planning of the Christian denominations. My object in this second chapter is to ask why this is so — with special reference to Protestant churches within our own North American context. Why are we still so thoroughly wedded to Christendom that we refuse to entertain consciously this great transition through which we are passing, and therefore fail to engage in the kind of radical reassessment and reforming of our calling, our mission, our structures and ministries that would enable us, perhaps, to pass through this paradigm shift with greater self-understanding and a more faithful and imaginative kind of obedience?

The Dilemma of the Liberal and Moderate Churches at the End of Christendom

Although there are exceptions, it seems to me that most Christian denominations and congregations in our context are trying to behave as if nothing had happened — as if we were still living in a basically Christian civilization; as if the Christian religion were still quite obviously the official religion of the official culture; as if we could carry on baptizing, marrying, and burying everybody as we have always done; as if governments would listen to us, and educational institutions would respect us, and the general public would (perhaps begrudgingly) heed our moral and other pronouncements, and so on and so on, "world without end." Many denominations mount specific programs to deal with this or that "new" issue; but few want to pay any attention to the big issue, which is whether this imperial form of the Christian religion can even survive — or should! A sort of repressed or suppressed sense of failure eats away at the denominations, often manifesting itself openly in economic and leadership crises. But instead of addressing this forthrightly, we live with it at the subconscious level and, in the meantime, get on with schemes to keep the status quo going as long as possible.

We still want to tell the Christian story as a success story — that is, in much the same way as we heard it in the segments that I quoted in the first chapter — documents from the earlier part of the century telling of the progressive triumph of the Christian religion over all obstacles, rivals, and alternatives. Ironically, much of the this-worldly triumphalism of early twentieth-century liberalism has been adapted to the language and methods of evangelical fundamentalism, so that the missionary enthusiasm characterizing nineteenth-century liberal accounts of the Christian future, with their sense of the imminent arrival of the divine "Kingdom," is perhaps more frequently found today in militantly conservative Christian circles. Many self-defined evangelical Christians look to the twenty-*first* century in rather the same way liberals looked to the twentieth — as "The Christian Century."

As for the more liberal and moderate churches, the situation is decidedly complex. Vague reminiscences of the Kingdom-theology and missiology of liberalism are rhetorically present still in Anglican, Presbyterian, Lutheran, United, and the other denominations of this category. Such reminiscences are all but unavoidable in hymns ("Jesus shall reign where'er the sun . . .) and traditional prayers, and they hover about in the general ethos and collective memory of these denominations. But they are countered by new trends that have affected moderate and liberal Christianity in particular. These new trends have guaranteed that among liberal Christians today there would be not only less enthusiasm for Christian world conquering, but a frank suspicion of the whole idea. In fact, I would judge that the liberal and moderate denominations are characterized today by a palpable missiological confusion. The old liberalism with its enthusiasm for the ringing in of the divine Kingdom is now countered by a new liberalism that insists upon the rights of individuals to embrace whatever beliefs they choose. Let us examine this more closely.

This new liberalism belongs to the liberal mentality represented by and fostered within the Christian denominations whose members value sensitivity to the opinions and practices of others. This property of liberalism has made these denominations both conscious of and open to the realities of religious pluralism. The earlier, theoretical tolerance in liberal doctrine, which did not prevent liberal Protestant missionaries from assuming the superiority of Christianity over other faiths, has been compelled by the demographic realities of our present context to express itself more consistently in practical terms. These "other faiths" are no longer impersonal statistics descriptive of far-off lands, whose social condition may indeed have been worsened by religious practices that served the interests of the powerful; on the contrary, many practitioners of these faiths are citizens of our own cities and towns, people with whom we work, the parents of our children's playmates. The clear superiority of Christianity could be maintained by our Christian forebears more readily than by us, because the religions in comparison with which Christianity could be thought superior did not have faces and voices; they were in fact very abstract affairs. Their teachings, usually reduced and frequently caricatured, could without difficulty be shown to produce questionable moral and political effects. But the very liberalism that in the first place induced Christian people to undertake "comparative" studies of religion also conditioned them, as practitioners of non-Christian religions began to penetrate our own society, to open their minds and hearts to these strangers. Then, almost universally, they could no longer endorse even the less doctrinaire liberal versions of Christian missiology. Christian missionary endeavor, especially "foreign missions," is part of the ecclesiastical experience of everyone whose association with mainstream Protestantism reaches back four or five decades. Today it is rarely pursued with any enthusiasm in most congregations of these same denominations. The liberal temperament today can endorse foreign *aid* and global *service,* but not foreign *missions* and global *evangelism;* for the latter seems inseparable from white Western imperialism that liberal Christians, among others, have learned to regret and suspect.

No one with a modicum of Christian humanity can fault liberalism for having in this way made the world of the late twentieth century a little less parochial and violent than it would have been. But this laudable moral effect does not obviate the confusion that it has left in the once-mainline churches with respect to their identity and their purpose. If it is not the vocation of Christians to convert everyone to Christian faith, to expand the church's sphere of influence and its territory, and so to grow and prosper in every way as the doorway to the divine Kingdom, then what is our vocation, and what sort of future can we expect and work for?

In a word, "What are churches *for?*" This question hovers over our liberal, moderate Protestant congregations like an unwelcome sword of Damocles. Having been denied blatant applications of Constantinian imperialism, and by now fearful that almost any sort of explicitly Christian witness is probably "politically incorrect," the most common answer that is presently given — implicitly — to this question is a form of concentration upon the congregation itself: The church's purpose is to be a fellowship, a "friendly church." In cities and towns that are large and impersonal, the church is a meeting place where people "get to know one another" and to "care." In the livelier congregations, programs are developed for every age and stage of life. The Christian community should not be centered in itself alone: that does not make for good community spirit, nor does it accord with the dictates of Christian charity. So there should be outreach into the surrounding community, and social programs, and involvement in current ethical and social issues. Strangers making their way into the fellowship should be welcomed, and they should be encouraged to attend — because of the fellowship. But only rarely, it is felt, would it be appropriate to approach others as disciples of a quite explicit faith tradition. Even Christian preaching must honor the rights of others to believe what they will; therefore the proclamatory, or kerygmatic, dimension must be muted, and even the apologetic approach, which is preferable, must observe the primacy of personal choice.

Where this fellowship model of the church is successful (and that, in practice, I have observed, means largely in suburban settings), it can forestall the open articulation of the many questions that it begs. There are indeed more than enough human needs in our social arena to ensure that any organization exercising sensitivity and imagination in meeting them can find a place for itself. Moreover (lest this be taken as a purely critical commentary on such communities), let it be recognized that such congregations often perform admirable and profoundly humane services in our society. It may even be said that these services are Christian services, inspired by Christian ideals of love, hospitality, and tolerance.

But Christians are called not only to serve their neighbors but to confess their faith — their reasons for serving; and from that perspective it must be admitted that, just here, we are close to the center of a — of perhaps the — problem. How shall the churches that are most representative of the liberal and moderate Christian traditions of tolerance and sensitivity to the rights of others be communities of *Christ's discipleship?* — not only of *fellowship,* but of *discipleship?* — not only of *behavior* that may be regarded as Christian but also of Christian *confession?* Given the realities of pluralism and the democratic recognition of human freedom and dignity for which, among other things, these same Christian denominations have struggled, will it not constitute a violation of the very spirit of tolerant faith actually to *confess* the faith?

This is of course the question that is constantly flung at moderate and liberal Christian churches by the more biblically and doctrinally oriented denominations. It is regularly dismissed by liberal Christians as typical of biblicists of conservative faith. But although that rejoinder is usually true, it is hardly adequate as a response to the problem in question. To take the question seriously does not mean to adopt the attitudes, beliefs, and practices of those who ask it, and it certainly does not mean to take up their answers. Fundamentalist evangelicalism may have retained greater contact with Christendom's typical self-image, including its theology and missiology, but precisely for that reason its conception of the purpose and future of the church is more questionable than that of liberal and moderate Christianity. The liberals and moderates may at least in some real sense, in their best expressions, be living the faith; and faith's confession should not be reduced to verbal (and certainly not to rote doctrinal) confession. At the same time, however, the confession of the faith does have an indispensable verbal, ideational, intellectual connotation. Therefore, even if the fellowship and community outreach of the once-mainline churches can be construed as an implicit confession of the faith, the question remains why they are so seemingly incapable of giving a reason for the hope that is in them — so bereft of theology, so unsure and incapable of "gospel."

Another factor in the condition of these liberal and moderate churches has begun to manifest itself strongly: their quantitative depletion is at least partly the consequence of just this qualitative lack. Concentration upon fellowship, even when this is augmented by social activism and community concern and involvement, has definite limits. Its success as a *raison d'être* is largely dependent upon its location among a constituency that places a high premium upon such fellowship; hence, its strong identification with suburban, racially and economically homogenous churches. Denominations dominated by the middle classes tend to assume that this model of the church is viable everywhere, but it is clearly not viable in urban or even suburban settings where, for a variety of reasons, fellowship is either not a priority or less easily achieved. Even where the friendly church model seems successful, closer examination will reveal that its success is often superficial. In time, the friendly church wears thin. Those who are looking for meaning (and that is the most gripping search of humanity in our context) are not likely to find it in such churches. For one thing, part of the secret of their being reputedly friendly is their consistent avoidance of deeper human concerns, which are usually divisive. A superficial friendliness is no substitute for depth of meaning, or even of genuine community.

The fellowship model of the congregation reached its height in the 1950s, a period that witnessed new, postwar forms of enthusiasm for the American Dream and its paler Canadian version. Since that time, the character of public life in our context has become far more problematic. The answers that fellowship-Christianity provided to human needs are inadequate to the questions that have arisen in the postwar decades. The depletion of mainstream churches seems directly related, I believe, to this discrepancy.

Not surprisingly, the response to these losses that appears to have become the most popular among the denominations under discussion is "church growth." Church growth has appeal to the moderate and liberal Christian churches for an obvious reason; namely, it belongs to the mentality of the business and professional world — and of capitalism — which is based on the idea of growth. So the application of the growth concept to diminishing congregations can seem the most obvious way of rectifying their problems. Members of such congregations understand these tactics well, for they are part of the world to which the members belong.

The advocates of church growth can also depend upon a long tradition of Christian thinking about the role and future of the church. I refer, of course, to the Christendom model, which in various ways has also — as we saw in the first chapter — exploited the idea of continuous expansion. Doctrinal and even biblical authority can be found to support such programs. And of course the great advantage of this approach is that it demands nothing at all by way of a rethinking of the vocation of the church. It simply applies to the dominant model of the past contemporary techniques for achieving the same result, or better.

But how does church growth make itself compatible with the new liberalism? The old liberals could endorse Christian missionary endeavor because they believed in the superiority of their "product" over all others. The new liberals cannot permit themselves to engage in programs of Christian expansion that ride roughshod over the freedoms and rights of others. The answer usually given is: Church growth concentrates on the disenchanted and backsliding among those who would have been Christians had they not opted for or been seduced by secularity.

The Tenacity of Cultural Establishment

The conclusion to be drawn from this analysis of responses to the humiliation of Christendom at work in American and Canadian churches is that few Christians seem ready to let go of the Constantinian model of the church. Fundamentalists and conservatives have perhaps inherited the more blatant forms of Christian missionary imperialism, but the moderate and liberal denominations give little evidence of being prepared to entertain any other model in a radical way, despite their missiological confusion. Their own liberal-democratic consciousness having prevented them from perpetuating the expansionist evangelism of the liberal and moderate Protestant traditions, they either simply fail to come to grips with the changed circumstances in which they find themselves, or else they opt for methods, like "church growth," which permit them to exploit the old, more sedate forms of Constantinianism a little longer without impinging too conspicuously on the qualms of new liberals respecting Christian exclusivity. Although there are significant minorities in all the liberal and moderate denominations of Protestantism who are seeking alternative ways of conceiving of the nature and purpose of the church, the majority appear prepared to attempt to carry on business as usual. This approach is still possible in many places in our North American context, and here and there it can even seem successful; but it is both shortsighted in practical terms and, in my view, theologically questionable.

Why is there such reluctance to recognize this great transition through which the Christian movement is passing? Why do Christians in our context so consistently resist the opportunities for genuine discipleship that historical providence has opened to us just at this point? Why, when even at the center of these same congregations there is a palpable sense of dissatisfaction and boredom with ecclesiastic business as usual, do we still go through the motions? The reason — or one important part of it — is that the form of Christian establishment that has characterized the history of our two countries is inherently a tenacious one. Let me explain what I mean.

The establishment of the Christian religion in both Canada and the United States, particularly the latter, has been infinitely more subtle and profound than anything achieved in the European parental cultures. The reason for this is not very complicated. It is that whereas the old, European forms of Christian establishment were legal ones (*de jure*), ours have been cultural, ideational, social (*de facto*). Or, to put it in another way, whereas the traditional establishments of European Christendom were at the level of *form*, ours have been at the level of *content*.

One suspects that our very refusal of *formal* patterns of Christian establishment has blinded us to the power of our *informal*, culture-religion pattern. In both Canada and the

United States, there have always been influential voices reminding us of the separation of church and state. But only rather recently have a few voices alerted us to the paradoxical manner in which, while disclaiming any official ties with government, representatives of the Christian religion could always assume highly if not exclusively favorable attitudes toward Christianity on the part not only of most citizens but also of officialdom. Søren Kierkegaard's critical witness against Christendom in mid-nineteenth century Europe was coterminous with what Sidney Mead, the dean of American church historians, identified as the point at which Christianity and Americanism became merged into a unified sort of spirituality. Mead wrote that "during the second half of the nineteenth century there occurred an ideological amalgamation of [denominational] Protestantism with 'Americanism,' and . . . we are still living with some of the results" (Mead 1963:134). But Kierkegaard (1813–55) would not have known, I suspect, what to say in the face of a Christian establishment in the New World that had refused the status of legality and was, partly for that very reason, all the more entrenched socially and even, in a hidden way, legally.

The tenacity of the North American cultural establishment of Christianity is evident today as both Europe and North America encounter the effects of Christendom's decline. It is interesting to notice the quite different ways in which Western European churches and North American churches have responded to the process of secularization and ecclesiastical reduction. On the whole, I feel, the Europeans have managed this transition much more gracefully than we. One cannot admire everything that is transpiring in European Christianity today — certainly not the presumptuous hope, entertained in some high quarters, that, now that Marxist states have failed,

Christendom may reclaim exclusive cultic rights to its old European home. But one can admire the way in which many European Christians, western and eastern, have accepted the new, minority status of believing Christianity and have experienced this as both release and opportunity: release from the duties of chaplaincy to authority; opportunity for truer, untrammeled service of God and creation.

What this contrast demonstrates is the deep-rootedness of Christian establishment, North American style. Legal arrangements such as those between various European states and state-churches, even if they have lasted for centuries, are set aside with relative ease as soon as both parties desire it or (what is more likely) the stronger party, the state, no longer benefits from it. There are religious "leftovers," of course: church taxes may still be collected and (as in western Germany) most people still dutifully pay them (though this is now rapidly changing in Germany); state occasions, like the coronation of British monarchs, still require religious pomp and sanction, though who knows what the next coronation (if there is one) will be! Nevertheless, it is relatively clear to Europeans where the line is drawn between serious faith and civic cultus. With us in North America, on the contrary, Christ and culture are so subtly intertwined, so inextricably connected at the subconscious or unconscious level, that we hardly know where one leaves off and the other begins. The substance of the faith and the substance of our cultural values and morality appear, to most real or nominal Christians in the United States and Canada, virtually synonymous.

In short, our New World variety of Christian establishment has the enormous staying power that it has because it is part and parcel of our whole inherited system of meaning, a system combining Judeo-Christian, Enlightenment, Romanticidealist, and more recent nationalistic elements so intermingled that even learned persons have difficulty distinguishing them. One cannot judge ordinary people, therefore, who equate "un-Christian" and "un-American" sentiments.

Given this identification of "Christ and culture" (to use H. R. Niebuhr's categories), it is understandable that the average North American churchgoer finds it confusing in the extreme to entertain the more critical interpretation of the Christian past that much historical and theological scholarship is offering today; for this necessarily entails entertaining a less positive assessment, as well, of his or her nation's past. And if it is hard for such persons to accept another rendition of the *past,* it is even harder for them to conceive of a *future* that may be fundamentally discontinuous with that idealized past. It is true that in some of the traditions springing from the radical wing of the Reformation the idea of a Christian community separate and distinct from the majority culture can still achieve a hearing; but in the once-mainline denominations of the continent the thought that the Christian identity and vocation would require a deliberate distancing of the church from the pursuits and values of dominant society is still, it would seem, so foreign an idea as to be ungraspable even at the intellectual level. Emotionally speaking, such a thought is for most North Americans simply un-American or un-Canadian; that is, un-Christian.

What I will suggest in the next chapter, however, is that if Christians today and tomorrow want to preserve the faith and not just some of its moral and aesthetic spin-off, they are going to have to become more articulate about their basic beliefs and about the manner in which these beliefs, when taken seriously, distance them from many of the values and pursuits of our society at large. We are being pushed to the edges of our society as churches; that is to say, we are being disestablished. The question is whether we can assume some active role in this process instead of simply letting it happen to us. What would it mean to disestablish ourselves?

On that question, a Christian denomination that has its historic link with the Anabaptist traditions could be of enormous help to the rest of us — provided they, too, are ready to search their hearts and minds to distinguish what is best in their tradition from the sorts of cultural establishments that they also may have been tempted to entertain.

In the next two chapters, having tried in the initial two to characterize what I regard as the major ecclesiastical problem confronting Christians in the post-Christendom situation, I will attempt to describe in more positive terms how I feel we ought to respond to this problem.

3

Intentional Disestablishment:
A Work of Theology

I believe that the phase of the Christian movement that we call Christendom (i.e., the domination of official Christianity in the Western world) is coming — has come — to an effective end, despite vestiges of Christendom that continue today and may continue for a long time. I also find that the Christian churches or denominations are resisting this ending mightily, mostly by repressing their actual awareness of it. One reason why it is possible to do this in the North American situation is that our kind of establishment on this continent has been cultural rather than legal; that is, it has been an identification of Christianity with general social values and mores of the dominant classes. This has meant that Christianity has been able to seem viable as the majority faith in North America longer than in most of the older, legally established European church situations.

However, I believe that, appearances to the contrary, we North American churches are also now being pushed visibly to the periphery. And the question is: Are we just going to let this happen *to* us, or can we give some concrete direction to this process of disestablishment? Can we make it work for good? Not because I am an optimist but because I believe in God, I will suggest that we can. We can in some meaningful sense disestablish *ourselves* and in the process recover something of our genuine mission in the world. In the final chapter, I will characterize that genuine mission as the mission of a prophetic minority — salt, yeast, and light — distinct from the social milieu of which it is part, yet assuming a new kind of responsibility for its host society and for the evolving of God's creation.

The Reality of Our Disestablishment

Despite the tenacity of our establishment, a process of disestablishment has been under way in the United States and Canada for some time — at least since the end of World War II. Hence, an effective distancing from the dominant culture is occurring quite apart from any determination on the part of the church bodies concerned. We are no longer mainline churches or major denominations in anything but the historical sense of having grown out of older families of Christendom. We are not mainstream churches if that term implies, as it does for most people, a certain social status: a status of unquestionable social respectability; a status of right-thinking American Christianity; a status of being accepted as the unofficial-official cultus of our dominant culture. We may be allowed to play that role here and there, but I think we are deluded if we imagine that it is a role that our society reserves for us alone, one that will simply be held open for us, world without end! I do not claim that we are socially insignificant; in fact, I believe that we have a greater potentiality for genuine public significance now than we have actually had in the past.

But for the moment my point is only that most of the denominations which formerly could claim for themselves such distinctions as mainline or mainstream or major denomination are undergoing a shift to the periphery.

This shift is partly (but only partly) made conspicuous at the quantitative level. According to the recent study *Christianity: A Social and Cultural History,* "most of the denominations that dominated America's religious life before the Civil War (Congregationalists, Episcopalians, Presbyterians, and Methodists) are in decline" (Kee et al. 1991:731). Between the years 1940 and 1986, there was an increase in the population of the United States from 130 million to over 240 million, a rise of 83 percent. "Denominations defined by their European origins — for example, Lutherans and Mennonites — have grown at rates roughly comparable to the rise in population. Most of the older Protestant denominations have had rates of growth considerably below the rise in population, and some of the mainline denominations actually lost membership in the 1970's and 1980's" (ibid.).

The American ecclesiastical situation, quantitatively speaking, is of course more impressive (I'd say deceptively impressive) than that of Europe; but it would be naive to imagine that North America will continue to differ markedly from Europe in this respect. According to the 1982 edition of the exhaustive *World Christian Encyclopedia,* "White Westerners cease to be practicing Christians at a rate of 7,600 per day" (Barrett 1982). John Taylor, in an essay entitled "The Future of Christianity" in the recent *Oxford Illustrated History of Christianity,* remarks: "There is no society more saturated with Christian influence. Yet the main thrust of that steep rise in the number of people in the world who are without religion...has occurred, not under anti-religious despotism, but in Western Europe" (Taylor 1990:657). Hans Küng's one-sentence summary of the global situation seems generally accurate: "Of the three billion inhabitants of the earth, only about 950 millions are Christian and only a fraction of those take any practical part in the church" (1986:195–99).

Although statistics are not to be scoffed at by Christian thinkers, they do not, however, tell the whole story. The effective disestablishment of Christianity in its traditional Western form is experienced by all of us at levels of recognition that go deeper than our knowledge of church membership rolls, finances, and other readily quantifiable data. If we have lived in North America for fifty or sixty years, then, unless we are among the exceptions, we have witnessed the advent of public attitudes toward religion that are vastly different from those that were prevalent in our teens and twenties. Not only have we seen the rapid growth of an almost complete religionless-ness on the part of many of our contemporaries; not only have we observed the erection, in our towns and cities, of temples, mosques, and pavilions of faiths known to us formerly, if they were known at all, only out of storybooks of our youth; not only have we lived to see the proliferation of Christian sectarian groups and (what is more unnerving to us) their elevation to high social visibility and even (in the public mind) to the status of normative Christianity; not only have we observed, accordingly, how the instinct to belief, if there is such a thing, may now satisfy itself in literally thousands of ways that have little or nothing to do with the Christianity that we took for granted in, say, 1948; but beyond all that the discriminating among us have discerned the appearance of new attitudes toward the whole phenomenon of religion: that it is strictly an option; that it is a purely individual decision; that there is no reason why the children of believing parents should be considered potential members of religious communions; that religion may be useful, but truth does not apply to this category, and so on.

Such nonquantifiable experiences as these, and not only the statistics, were undoubtedly in the mind of the American church historian Robert T. Handy, when in the final chapter of his 1977 book, *A History of the Churches in the United States and Canada,* he wrote:

> The American and Canadian churches entered the period following World War I devoted as they had always sought to be to the services of God and to the continuation of the patterns of western Christendom. . . .
>
> In the half century following World War I increasing numbers of persons both inside and outside the churches came to believe that their civilization was no longer basically Christian and that Christendom was a fading reality (:377).

The question with which such observations leave us is not whether we can or cannot continue to assume the supposed privileges of our historical form of establishment; rather, it is whether we will simply allow the process of being disestablished happen to us or whether, as individuals and Christian bodies, we will take some active part in directing the process. The process itself, I believe, cannot be reversed; moreover, I do not believe that Christ's discipleship is well served by trying to reverse it. The scramble to regain, or retrieve, or recreate Christendom, which is entertained in various forms and programs by several powerful Christian lobbies in North America and beyond, seems to me both socially naive and theologically questionable. Even if it could be achieved (and it could not be achieved without violence, psychological if not physical), it would not represent a faithful reading of "gospel" for our context.

Those who do entertain the idea of re-Christianizing the West would do well to consider more carefully the millennium and a half during which the Christian religion did dominate Europe and its satellites. I think that church historians, who have tended during our own time to be academicians distanced from the pursuits of the institutional churches, have a particularly important role to play in ecclesiastical life today. Whatever else the study of history may mean, it entails the pursuit of truth about the past, and therefore it functions critically in relation to the tendency of institutions to indulge in one-sided and romantic versions of their own historical foundations and progress. A church history sensing its responsibility to the church in our context — a context in which there is a temptation to attempt to recover Christendom's allegedly glorious past — is obliged to keep before the churches the memory of what it was necessary for them to do and to become in order to achieve the state of preeminence. In particular, such historians would be required to study and communicate in detail the history of Christian attitudes of every kind. Whoever thinks that Jesus Christ commands his "Body" to convert everyone to an explicitly Christian faith had better contemplate the long, sad, and often gruesome story of Christian anti-Judaism. Whoever believes that Christian mission means Christian expansion had better reconsider the terrible devastations wrought in the Americas by Europe's various Christian "conquerors."

If, then, we find ourselves among those who can neither pretend that nothing has changed, nor ignore the whole situation, nor seek to reconstitute the Humpty-Dumpty that was Christendom; and if at the same time we are not content simply to allow the process of disestablishment to happen to us, then the only alternative that remains is to accept the reality of our new situation, to look for the positive possibilities that it presents, and to seek to give meaningful direction to what historical providence appears to have in store for us.

We could, of course, simply fall into despair. Many have already opted for that choice — quietly, for the most part. One can understand their discouragement. But finally it is not necessary. Given a modicum of grace and imagination, thinking Christians today can prepare themselves to see precisely in our disestablishment, not an impersonal and inglorious destiny such as may be the fate of any institution, but the will and providence of God. Our Protestant traditions of theology insist that God is at work in history, and that the divine Spirit creates, recreates, judges, and renews the "body of Christ." What is happening to the churches of Europe and North America today cannot, therefore, be received by us as if it were devoid of purpose. The hand of God is in it!

Disestablishing *Ourselves!*

But our Protestant traditions of theology also insist that God's hand reaches out to the human counterpart, the covenant partner. History, including the history of the church, when it is Christianity understood, should never be conceived of as that which willy-nilly happens *to* human beings and societies. Even though Christians must reject the modern idea that humans are the autonomous makers of history, the covenantal basis of our faith places upon humankind a participatory responsibility for the unfolding of God's purposes. Christians understand themselves to be stewards of the mysteries of God (1 Cor. 4:1). Accordingly, we are called to participate in the judg-

ment that begins at the household of faith (1 Pet. 4:17), and
to participate also in the re-forming of that household. The
Reformation teaching concerning the continuous reformation
of the disciple community (*semper reformanda*) assumes that
God permits and commands the church to be involved in its
own self-assessment and change, and that when this does not
occur something of the very essence of the church has been
forfeited.

When, therefore, in the subheading of the second sec-
tion of this chapter I affirm that the message of the divine
Spirit to the churches in Canada and the United States is,
"Disestablish yourselves!" I am referring to just that kind of
participation and stewardship. Divine Providence is offering
us another possibility, a new form, indeed a new life. But
we may accept this gift of the new only as we relinquish the
old to which we are stubbornly clinging. We may reform ourselves according to the new form that is God's possibility for
us only as we intentionally relinquish the social status that
belongs to our past: the comfortable relationships with governments and ruling classes; the continuous confirmation of
accepted social values and mores by means of which we sus-
tain those relationships; the espousal of "charities" that ease
our guilty consciences while allowing us to maintain neutrality
with respect to the social structures that make such "charities"
necessary; the silent acceptance of racial, sexual, gender, and
economic injustices, or their trivialization through tokenism;
the failure to probe the depths of human and creaturely pathos
by confining sin to petty immorality or doctrinal refinements
drawn from the past, and so on. There is still largely unex-
plored wisdom in the tradition of Jerusalem, which, were we
to awaken to it, could enable the Christian church truly to engage our society at the heart of its crises. But we will not even

be awakened to that wisdom so long as we are content to play the redundant role of official religious cult in our society.

The point is, however, that that role is being snatched from us in any case, and the perpetuation of such an image of ourselves is in consequence increasingly pathetic. If we simply wait for more and more of the alleged privileges of establishment to be taken from us by societal forces over which we have little control, we will not even save for the future what was good in our past. If on the other hand we disengage *ourselves;* if with courage and trust we release our hold on what we have been conditioned to believe was our right, or an immutable form of the church; if, to use a newer Testamental image, we lose our life, ecclesiastically speaking, then we may in fact gain our life as Christ's living body.

At this juncture in our sojourn, *intentionality* is the key to the future that these old ecclesial structures may have.

Disengagement as a Work of Theology

Having established the necessary background thought, I will now seek to demonstrate the thesis that in my view must be seriously contemplated by all who remain in the once-mainline churches of these nations. That thesis may be stated as follows: Intentional *disengagement* from the dominant culture with which, in the past, the older Protestant denominations of this continent have been bound up is the necessary precondition for a meaningful *engagement* of our society, more particularly of that same dominant culture.

The demonstration of this thesis requires three steps. First, I must clarify what is entailed in an intentional disengagement from the dominant culture. Second, I must explain in a general way how such a disengagement could facilitate meaningful reengagement of that same culture. And third, I must provide enough concrete examples of such a process to give it contextual credibility. These tasks will occupy what remains of the present chapter, as well as the fourth and final chapter of this volume.

First, what is entailed in an intentional disengagement from the dominant culture? It is one thing to respond to such a question in societies, such as most European societies have been, where Christian establishments are of the legal variety. It is something else to do so in our North American context where, as I argued earlier, what obtains is a cultural establishment. Just because ours is an establishment more of content than of form; just because our close ties with the dominant culture have existed at the level of fundamental beliefs, lifestyles, and rudimentary moral assumptions, any effective extrication of ourselves from this by now severely limiting relationship has to occur at a more subtle level — that is to say, the level of thought. To put it quite clearly, for North American Christians who are serious about re-forming the church so that it may become a more faithful bearer of gospel in our social context, there is no alternative to a disciplined, prolonged, and above all critical work of theology. By this I do not mean merely academic theology, but a theology that reaches into the life of congregations; a theology that asks of every Christian something of what it asks of those who pursue it as a lifework or calling. In short, by theology I mean what Luther had in mind when he wrote, *Vivendo, immo moriendo et damnando fit theologus, non intelligendo, legendo aut speculando* ("It is by living — no rather, by dying and being damned — that a theologian is made, not merely by understanding, reading or speculating" [WA 5.163.28]).

Concretely speaking, Christians must learn how to distinguish the Christian message from the operative assumptions, values, and pursuits of our host society, and more particularly those segments of our society with which, as so-called mainstream churches, we have been identified. Because most of the denominations in question are bound up with middle-class, Caucasian, and broadly liberal elements of our society, what we will have to learn is that the Christian message is not just a stained-glass version of the worldview of that same social stratum.

This is of course easily said. In these days, it is also said rather frequently. But I am not convinced that it has been grasped by more than a small percentage of Protestant clergy and laity. Moreover, the movements in our midst that have taken seriously the need for Christians in North America to distance themselves from the worldview of their conventional socioeconomic constituency seem to me to err, often, in two fundamentals ways. First, some of these voices convey the impression that such distancing is the very goal for which we should strive, and not just a means to our more authentic reengagement of this same society. They give many indications of disliking this social stratum and everything that it stands for. They often seem to assume that First World, white, middle-class societies are by definition irredeemable; that they are driven by an irreversible logic of oppression, injustice, and racial exclusivity. They tell us, in one way or another, that our only salvation as Christians is to dissociate ourselves from our WASPish past (or whatever its equivalent in Germanic, Scandinavian, and other terms) and to align ourselves instead with those whom we oppress.

One can understand the peculiar vehemence of such persons, especially those among them who know, profoundly, the plight of the victims of our society. But the abandonment of the oppressor is not very likely a way of effecting change. Besides, as Wendy Farley of Emory University has aptly stated, for those adopting this approach,

> sensitivity to injustice and suffering often becomes a new dualism that categorizes human beings according to membership in the group of the oppressed or the oppressor....
>
> I am not convinced that this objectification of humanity into victim and executioner does justice to the complexity of the human individual or to the dynamic of evil.... The web that unites victim and tyrant in the same person is more complex than the white hat/black hat caricature that seems banal even in its natural habitat, the "grade B" movie (Farley 1990:51–52).

The second questionable way in which minorities in the once-mainline churches try to re-form the churches is by identifying "true Christianity" with the adoption of what are perceived as radical positions on various contemporary issues of personal and social ethics. They insist that Christianity means advocating economic reforms aimed at greater global justice, or full-scale disarmament, or the preservation of species, or gender equality, or racial integration, and so on. I am entirely in agreement with the ethical conclusions suggested here, but they are conclusions, not points of departure. Perhaps the presentation of a radical ethic of economic justice, for example, can be a catalyst, sometimes, for genuine Christian evangelism; but on the whole, it seems to me, profoundly altered moral attitudes and specific ethical decisions are consequences of the hearing of the gospel. When they are presented as if they were immediately accessible to everyone as categorical imperatives, so to speak, gospel and law are being confused.

The recent publication, *Christianity: A Social and Cultural History,* to which earlier reference has been made, draws attention to one of the unfortunate consequences of this confusion in contemporary Protestant churches:

> The difficulties of the older Protestant denominations may stem from their willingness to embrace ideas and trends as defined by the nation's media and educational elites, elites that are remarkably unrepresentative of the religion, politics, and values of the nation's population (Kee et al. 1991:734).

What I am seeking to establish by criticizing these two positions is that insofar as we are committed to genuine renewal in the churches that we represent, there are no shortcuts: *we must begin with basics.* We have two or three generations of people in and around the churches now who are, most of them, not only unfamiliar with the fundamental teachings of the Christian traditions but ignorant even of the Scriptures. Some denominations have been more diligent than others in the area of Christian education, but I doubt that any North American Protestant denomination stemming from the central streams of the Reformation could measure up to the minimal standards of catechesis assumed by the sixteenth-century reformers. We have even to ask ourselves whether we have a well-educated professional ministry, or at least a ministry whose basic theological education is continuously renewed and supplemented, and then incorporated into preaching and congregational leadership.

Without a deeper understanding of what Christians profess, it is absurd to think that ordinary church folk will be able to distinguish what is true to the Judeo-Christian tradition from the amalgam of religious sentimentalism and "bourgeois transcendence" (Käsemann) by which both church and culture are saturated. Until a far greater number of churchgoing Americans and Canadians have become more articulate about the faith than they currently are, we cannot expect the churches to stand back from their sociological moorings far enough to detach what Christians profess from the mishmash of modernism, postmodernism, secularism, pietism, and free-enterprise democracy with which Christianity in our context is so fantastically interwoven.

But that such a "right dividing of the word of truth" (2 Tim 2:15, KJV) is what we will have to aim for is borne out by recent sociological studies as well as theological-ecclesiastical investigations. In their 1987 work entitled *American Mainline Religion: Its Changing Shape and Future,* Wade Clark Roof and William McKinney write:

> If a revived public church is indeed on the horizon, moderate Protestantism will play a key role in bringing it into being. This will require forms and qualities of leadership that have seldom been forthcoming from the protestant middle; a revitalized ecumenicity and new, bold *theological* affirmations are critical..., especially a theology that resonates with and gives meaning to the experience of middle Americans (:243).

Disengagement from our status of cultural establishment is primarily, then, a work of theology. Although this certainly constitutes *work* — for contemporary Protestants as a whole are not given to prolonged *thought* about the faith — it is also a necessity that is felt by significant minorities within all of the denominations concerned. Instead of catering so exclusively to what are usually described as "pastoral needs" (though the term often cloaks institutional busywork), ministers today are recalled to the teaching office. If the minister of the congregation is not herself or himself in some genuine sense a theologian, we cannot expect lay persons to reflect some measure of the sort of informed thoughtfulness that is needed if we, as church, are to find a way into the future.

To conclude: The opportunity that comes to serious Christians at the very point where Christianity seems to be in decline is an opportunity that has seldom presented itself in Christian history: namely, the opportunity actually to become the salt, yeast, and light that the newer Testament speaks of as the character of Christ's disciple community. To grasp this opportunity, however, we must relinquish our centuries-old ambition to be the official religion, the dominant religion, of the dominant culture. Ideationally, we must disengage ourselves from our society if we are going to reengage our society at the level of truth, justice, and love.

In the final chapter, I will take up this theme of disengaging in order to reengage, and in that way I hope to make concrete the proposal of these chapters, namely, that after Christendom the Christian movement may get on with being what, all along, it has been called to be — the cruciform body of Jesus Christ, a priestly and prophetic community of "the Way."

4

On Being Salt, Yeast, and Light: The Christian Movement in a Post-Christian Era

At the risk of overkill, I will state my primary thesis once more: Christianity has arrived at the end of its sojourn as the official, or established, religion of the Western world. The churches resist coming to terms with this ending because it seems so dismal a thing. But in Christian thinking, endings can also be beginnings; and if we are courageous enough to enter into this ending thoughtfully and intentionally, we will discover a beginning that may surprise us. The end of Christendom could be the beginning of something more nearly like the church — the disciple community described by the Scriptures and treasured throughout the ages by prophetic minorities.

That is the basic idea. And now I come to the final stage in my argument: If at the level of fundamental belief and lifestyle we disengage ourselves, as a Christian movement, from the dominant societies, classes, and institutions we have been for centuries trying to court, we may be able to serve those societies, classes, and institutions in ways far more faithful and more humanly needful than Christendom usually did.

An Ancient Dialectic:
"Not Of" yet "In"

The hypothesis that we are exploring here is that intentional disengagement from the dominant culture is the necessary prerequisite of Christian engagement, or reengagement, of that same culture. I have maintained, in the first place, that the work of detachment or disengagement is a theological work. The second step toward explicating the viability of the thesis involves asking how disengagement can facilitate authentic engagement. Is this not doubletalk?

I think not. In fact, the idea of "disengaging-in-order-to-engage" is by no means either contradictory or novel. Indeed, every meaningful relationship involves something like it, and not as a once-for-all movement but as a continuous process. If you are part of something — simply part of it — you cannot engage it. With what, on what basis, would you do so?

Interestingly, the converse is also true. If you are altogether distinct from a given entity, completely different, of another order altogether, then you cannot communicate with it. You lack the necessary connections, involvement, reciprocity. Genuine engagement of anything or anyone presupposes a dynamic of difference and sameness, distinction and participation, transcendence and mutuality.

Surely just such a relation is what the newer Testament has in mind when on the one hand it calls the disciple community to distinguish itself from the world (e.g., Rom. 12:2), and on the other, sends it decisively into the world (e.g., Matt. 28:19).

The New Testament expects the body of Christ to be all the more intensively *in* the world just because it is not simply *of* the world.

This same dialectic of separation and solidarity may be applied to the situation in which, as North American churches of the classical Protestant traditions, we find ourselves at this juncture in our historical pilgrimage. George Lindbeck, in his seminal book *The Nature of Doctrine,* has expressed our present ecclesiastical situation vis-à-vis our society in what I consider the clearest possible way. We are, he says, "in the awkwardly intermediate stage of having once been culturally established but . . . not yet clearly disestablished" (1984:134). In terms of the dialectic in question, the North American churches are both part of our culture and yet distinct, in it yet outside of it, or on the periphery looking in.

Now, given the almost unequivocal accord between Protestantism and middle-North Americanism that has characterized our past, the present duplicity of this relationship is indeed an awkward position for the churches to occupy. Therefore it is not surprising that our first inclination is to overcome it as soon as possible. Who wants to be awkward? Accordingly, Professor Lindbeck recognizes two ways, quite opposed to each other, in which Christians try to surpass their currently ambiguous state, socially and religiously.

One is the basically liberal theological inclination to attempt, in whatever ways one can, to present the Christian message in currently intelligible forms: that is, to bridge the gap between gospel and situation; to engage in an apologetic that will reinforce the ties of trust and cooperation between the church and the sociological segments with which, traditionally, we have made our bed. Here, in other words, the awkwardness is overcome by accentuating the dimension of participation and involvement. We are part of this dominant culture, and we intend by hook or by crook to keep our standing within it. To that end, we will sacrifice many things dear to the tradition. If the public wants peace of mind and friendly churches, then we will give them just that, and we will not ask any awkward questions or make any radical demands.

The other way of getting beyond the current awkwardness in the relations between "Christ and Culture" is to accentuate, on the contrary, the dimension of distance, difference, discontinuity. Lindbeck calls this the "postliberal" approach, though he explains that he intends that term to include such concepts as "postmodern," "postrevisionist," "postneoorthodox." The posture of this postliberal stance is kerygmatic rather than apologetic. According to this position, "Theology should . . . resist the clamor of the religiously interested public for what is currently fashionable and immediately intelligible. It should instead prepare for a *future* when continuing dechristianization will make greater Christian authenticity communally possible" (ibid.).

By these definitions, it will be obvious to you that there is an element of the latter (postliberal) approach in my interpretation "Disestablish yourselves!" At least I believe that the churches will have nothing to say to our culture, finally, if we simply take our cue from our society and fill its everchanging but always similar demands from the great supply house of our traditions, loosely interpreted. We must stand off from the liberal middle-class culture with which we have been consistently identified; rediscover our own distinctive ontological foundations and the ethical directives that arise from them; and allow ourselves, if necessary, to become aliens in our own land. In this, I am with Barth, the late William Stringfellow, and (perhaps) Stanley Hauerwas.[2]

Yet I am also uncomfortable with the approach of these theologians; for with representatives of the apologetic school of Christian theology I feel that the gospel was made for humanity — not just for some future humanity, to be addressed by some purer form of the church, but for human beings, sinners, here and now. And because I cannot find myself at home in either the liberal or the postliberal camps, as defined by Lindbeck, I question whether these are in fact the only alternatives available — indeed, whether we should admit the legitimacy of these two alternatives at all!

If it is true that we are in the position Lindbeck describes as awkward (and I think it is), then instead of trying to escape from the position by resolving it in one way or another, why should we not seek the positive and beneficial implications of such a position? Awkwardness may be an embarrassment to the urbane ecclesiastical mentality that wants always to be clear-cut; but it may also be part of being fools for Christ today.

What I mean is this: Could we not make the awkward relationship between the church and the dominant culture of our nations serve the Christian evangel? Could it not become a highly provocative situation — a modern application of the scriptural dialectic of being "in" yet not "of"?

Such a situation could serve the mission of the Christ of God in the world only insofar as we do sufficiently disengage ourselves from that world — intentionally, and not as pawns of an impersonal historical destiny. If we are faithful and imaginative enough to disentangle our authentic tradition of belief from its cultural wrapping, we will have something to bring to our world that it does not have — a perspective on itself, a judgment of its pretensions and injustices, an offer of renewal and hope. Only as a community that does not find its source of identity and vocation *within* its cultural milieu can the church acquire any intimations of "gospel" *for* its cultural milieu.

But although this postliberal sense of discontinuity with the liberal cultures of the United States and Canada is a necessary stage on the way to church renewal, it is only a stage. The end in relation to which it is a means is a new and existentially vital engagement of the same society from which it has to distinguish itself. And here, I think, the liberal insight is right: namely, that because, as liberal and moderate churches, we have known this particular segment of our society, having been part of it, we have both responsibility toward it and genuine potential for reengaging it. Our belonging to that so-called dominant culture, if it is still dominant, constitutes the dimension of reciprocity and continuity without which it would be very difficult, if not impossible, to achieve such a reengagement. Because we are also in some continuing way, most of us, "of" that white, middle-class, Protestant milieu, we know, from the inside, its questions, its anxieties, its frustrations, as well as its answers, consolations, and dreams. Our former establishment, which in the foreseeable future will still affect most of us at least at the psychic level, is thus not a complete loss, something to be regretted and shunned, but a long and deep historical experience from which, if we are sufficiently wise, much insight may be gained for the representation of the divine Word to that same world of expectation and experience. Indeed, if we did not have that knowledge and memory of our establishment, we would probably not be able to engage our world, no matter how stunning might be the message that we feel we have for it.

Four Worldly Quests — and Christian Witness

The third requirement of my thesis is to rescue it from abstraction by providing concrete illustrations of what is meant by disengaging-in-order-to-engage. I will do so by singling out four human quests that I feel are strongly present in the dominant culture of Canada and the United States today. I cannot develop any of these at length, but I will try to say enough about these quests to substantiate my basic point. In each case, I want to show two things: first, how our society longs for something that its performance regularly denies and its operative values frustrate, and second, how, as those who themselves participate in that longing, Christians may engage their society from the perspective of faith and hope. The four quests I will name as follows: (1) the quest for moral authenticity, (2) the quest for meaningful community, (3) the quest for transcendence and mystery, and (4) the quest for meaning.

The Quest for Moral Authenticity

The emphasis here should be placed on the word *authenticity.* I think that there is a quest for authentic, as distinct from conventional, morality strongly present in our society today. The reason for this is bound up with the failure of both the old and the so-called new moralities. People know now, better than they did in the 1960s and 1970s, that the permissiveness of the new morality leads to moral chaos and indeed to life-threatening dangers. AIDS has dramatized this, but it is visible everywhere — especially to those who have reason to care.

Thus the late Christopher Lash, in his book *The True and Only Heaven,* considers the world from the perspective of a caring parent:

To see the modern world from the point of view of a parent is to see it in the worst possible light. This perspective unmistakably reveals the unwholesomeness, not to put it more strongly, of our way of life: our obsession with sex, violence, and the pornography of "making it"; our addictive dependence on drugs, "entertainment," and the evening news; our impatience with anything that limits our sovereign freedom of choice, especially with the constraints of marital and familial ties; our preference for "nonbinding commitments"; our third-rate educational system; our third-rate morality; our refusal to draw a distinction between right and wrong, lest we "impose" our morality on others; our reluctance to judge or be judged; our indifference to the needs of future generations, as evidenced by our willingness to saddle them with a huge national debt, an overgrown arsenal of destruction, and a deteriorating environment; our unstated assumption, which underlies so much of the propaganda for unlimited abortion, that only those children born for success ought to be allowed to be born at all (1991:33–34).

Most of us who are members of the once-mainline churches, whether lay or clerical, are well-acquainted with this dilemma personally. We ourselves, as parents or teachers or simply as responsible citizens, know from the inside how difficult it is to experience anything approaching moral authenticity in the great, impersonal society of the workaday world. We hardly dare to examine our own lives, for we sense both their moral contradictions and their deep but largely unfulfilled longing for authenticity.

This, surely, is an integral aspect of our real participation in the world that, as Christians, we are called to engage. We know the moral confusion of this world because it is also our confusion. What, it seems to me, we have not yet fully grasped is that this very fact — our own participation in the anguished quest for moral authenticity — constitutes the apologetic point of contact without which we could not begin to reach out to others. Instead, therefore, of retreating into theological and ethical systems that only insulate us from the moral dilemmas of our contemporaries, we Christians must learn how to go to our Scriptures and traditions as bearers and representatives of those existential dilemmas. How does "gospel" address those who in our time and place "hunger and thirst for righteousness" — for moral integrity? How would Jesus speak to affluent young parents, caught between yuppidom and genuine concern for their children's future, and asking, like that young ruler who came to Jesus by night, how to be "good"? If we can identify with those parents (and we can!) then perhaps we will also begin to hear what our Lord would say to them. And I suspect that what we would hear would be something quite different from what is proffered by the television sitcoms.

The Quest for Meaningful Community

This quest, like the search for authentic morality with which it is closely related, is also conspicuous today because of a double failure — the failure of individualism and the failure of most forms of social cohesiveness.

The pursuit of individual freedom and personal aggrandizement has been the ideological backbone of new-world liberal society. It grew out of ancient constricting and oppressive forms of human communality, and it was never all bad. But we North Americans drove it to its absolute limits, and it takes little wisdom to recognize that this cannot continue to be the cornerstone of society. There have always been inherent contradictions here, and the contradictions have caught up with us. There is no significant problem of either private or public life that can be answered responsibly today by liberal individualism.

At the same time, we have witnessed the failure of most familiar forms of communality — dramatically so in Eastern Europe, but also in our own society, where a deep cynicism informs all public life and institutions. In cities that have become practically ungovernable, the profound alienation of persons is felt particularly by the elderly who, whatever relative success their active middle years may have brought them, must one way or another now, in their extremity, discover their dependence upon others.

In the churches that we represent, we are not unfamiliar with all this; most of us, too, as members and as ministers of churches, know about this double failure. Our very congregations, which are supposed to be the Christian answer to the human quest for genuine community (*koinonia*), are for many if not most churchgoers ingenuine, not to say artificial. And for those who do not fit the economic, educational, racial, or sexual mold that the churches still project, our congregations even accentuate the failure of community.

We participate, then, as middle-class Christians, in this quest; we know its terrible frustrations. But instead of allowing the specifics both of the quest and of its frustrations to challenge and inform our understanding and profession of the faith, we retreat into conventional answers. Because we do not permit the quest and the questions a significant place in our consciousness, we also fail to discern responses that, from the side of the tradition of Jerusalem, might indeed engage those who ask — including ourselves.

What would it mean to go to the Scriptures (e.g., to the Pauline metaphor of the body and its many members) with such contemporary experiences and questions fully present and articulated — not the familiar questions of generations of theological classrooms, but concrete questions, posed by the lives we know and honed into graphic forms by the best of our novelists, filmmakers, and social commentators? And would a congregation whose life and work were informed by such a meeting of text and context be satisfied, then, with the kind of community gathered for worship on Sunday mornings in towns and cities throughout North America, or at coffee hours after worship?

The Quest for Transcendence and Mystery

Several important theological books of the 1960s celebrated the secular city: at last we could see the world for what it was, without investing it with all sorts of semipantheistic holiness! But secularism too has failed. Technology, its most precocious offspring, began a decade or so ago to appear even to ordinary people the mixed blessing that some of the wise ones of the Western world already understood much earlier. During the past ten years — and primarily in the wake of the new environmental awareness — Western peoples have become newly conscious of the devastations of which humanity is capable when it thinks itself accountable to nothing beyond itself.

This realization, perhaps combined with the aboriginal human restlessness of which Augustine spoke in the first paragraph of the *Confessions,* has engendered in many a new and earnest search for some sense of transcendence and mystery. Many can now understand such judgments as that of Loren Eiseley, who spoke of human difference from other creatures not in the glowing terms of the Enlightenment (how we are "rational," capable of "free will," and so on), but on the contrary how this "different" creature, *homo sapiens,* "without the sense of the holy, without compassion," possesses a brain that can "become a gray stalking horror — the deviser of Belsen" (Wentz 1984:430).

Yet the quest for transcendence and mystery is constantly inhibited by the haunting awareness of our one-dimensionality. The "death of God" still dogs our footsteps. We try very hard to create depth, we speak much about in-depth analyses, and so forth. We would like to see ourselves against the backdrop of an eternity in which time is wonderfully enfolded. Everyone has learned the word spirituality. Yet it is not easy to overcome the rationalist impact of two centuries of Science — capital "S": "knowledge without love" (C. F. von Weizsäcker).

In the churches, too, we know these inhibitions. Try as we may, our services of worship bear about them the aura of the theater (mostly, I fear, of very amateur theater!), as though God were really dead and all that remained were our ritual performances for one another. Too often, these attempts at "divine service" (*Gottesdienst*) put one in mind of King Claudius in Shakespeare's *Hamlet:*

> My words fly up, my thoughts remain below:
> Words without thoughts never to heaven go.

> (Act III, Scene III)

Insofar as we allow ourselves as Christians to know, in all honesty, the longing and the dissatisfaction of this contemporary quest for transcendence and mystery, we are also in a position to respond to it out of the riches of the Judeo-Christian tradition, newly revisited with just these experiences in hand. Here and there, Christians are discovering how to discern the transcendent *within* the imminent — to see creation itself as mystery. But such discoveries depend upon a greater exposure to the bankruptcy of old familiar forms of spirituality than for the most part we have managed in our safe and sedate churches. We have been conditioned to look for God in "the beyond"; we are unaccustomed still to looking for "the beyond in the midst of life" (Bonhoeffer). Perhaps if we were to rethink our own tradition, bearing with us the terrible thirst for transcendence and mystery as it manifests itself in the soul of humanity *post mortem Dei,* we would more consistently discover the means for engaging it from the side of gospel.

The Quest for Meaning

Paul Tillich insisted that the basic anxiety type by which modern Western humanity is afflicted is the anxiety of meaninglessness and despair (Tillich 1952). For a time, it seems to me, the euphoria of secular humanism and technological experimentation blunted the edge of this anxiety. If, as the existentialists affirmed, we could not count on being heirs to a teleological universe, then we would create our own *telos,* our own essence. Many found that they could laugh at the old-fashioned search for the meaning of life. One of the most nihilistic films of the epoch capitalizes on this laughter: Monty Python's film *The Meaning of Life.*

But the laughter is hollow. A dimension of the alleged paradigm shift through which our culture is passing has to do precisely with the failure of that kind of anthropocentric bravado. All over the Western world there are covert and overt attempts to discover purpose — not a purpose we ourselves invent, but a horizon of meaning toward which we may turn and be saved. As Kurt Vonnegut says in one way or another in all of his strange and wonderful novels, perhaps cynically or perhaps seriously, purposeless things are abhorrent to the human species; and if the human species suspects that it is itself purposeless, it becomes conspicuously suicidal.

Under the now-more-conscious threat of nonbeing, humankind asks openly for the meaning of being. Religion is again interesting to many. And almost anything will do as the wherewithal for religion — shaped rocks that "put us in touch with the world-spirit," fire and smoke, silence, drumbeating, and so on.

Yet purpose is not easily located. The Religion of Progress, in its demise, has left a conspicuous vacuum, and there are strong withdrawal symptoms. The quasi-religious manner in which many, even among the intelligentsia, approach the computer and other marvels of communication indicates how difficult it is to let go of that religion and to face the void that letting go leaves.

Also, interestingly enough, the increase in demand for religions to fill the void left by ideological progress is accompanied by a marked decrease in those very churches that were formerly the cultic bulwarks of our culture. In those same churches, we who remain also know how hard it is to discover meaning for our lives, individually and corporately. We participate both in the quest for meaning and in its limits and defeats.

And therefore (therefore!) we may be in a position to rethink the basic things of our tradition in such a way as to discover in them that through which we may address our age with fresh insight and conviction. But this will be possible only if we expose ourselves less guardedly to the cold winds of the late twentieth century and are ready to carry its spiritual emptiness and yearning, with all the particularity thereto pertaining, into the presence of the Holy One. The Christian message may again speak to us, and make us ambassadors for Christ, if we appear before that One with empty hands — with the questions of those whom we, as priests of our neighbors, represent, which are also our questions — and wait for answers, or for the Answerer.

Conclusion

I began by asserting that it seems to me that the most urgent message of the divine Spirit to the churches in North America today is that they should disestablish themselves; for until they have learned to distinguish gospel from the rhetorical values, pretensions, and pursuits of the classes with which they are historically related, our churches will fail to detect, beneath the rhetoric of official optimism that still characterizes those classes, the actual humanity that it is our Christian vocation to address. In the service of the crucified one, who is as present in the largely hidden anxieties and oppressions of so-called First World peoples as he is in the more conspicuous sufferings of the poor and wretched of the earth, North American Christians must liberate themselves from the conventions of culture-religion.

Christian disengagement from the dominant culture is not to be confused, however, with the abandonment of that culture. The end that we are to seek is the redemption of our world — the world that is truly ours and of which we are ourselves part; the world described as "First," or "developed," which, despite its continuing bravado, has been given intimations of the judgment that the first may turn out to be last. Our role as Christians, as the people of the cross within that world, is precisely what Jesus said it was: to be salt, yeast, and light. Our Lord's metaphors for his community of witness were all of them modest ones: a little salt, a little yeast, a little light. Christendom tried to be great, large, magnificent. It thought *itself* the object of God's expansive grace; it forgot the meaning of its election to *worldly* responsibility.

Today we are constrained by the divine Spirit to rediscover the possibilities of littleness. We are to decrease in order that the Christ may increase. We cannot enter this new phase without pain, for truly we have been glorious in this world's own terms. It seems to many of us a humiliation that we are made to reconsider our destiny as "little flocks." Can such a calling be worthy of the servants of the Sovereign of the Universe?

Yet, if that Sovereign be the One who reigns from the cross, could any *other* calling be thought legitimate?

Notes

1. The author's main thesis is that the future toward which civilization is moving is one that will be characterized by human "dominion" over nature: "It will be a world in which Nature...will be truly 'humanized,' that is, dominated by the human will, and transvaluated to human uses" (Griffith-Jones 1926:307).

2. I qualify the latter support because Professor Hauerwas appears too often to court the kind of disengagement from the dominant culture that I have described earlier as being an end in itself. Perhaps he does not intend this, but his language frequently betrays a not-of-the-world posture so unqualified as to beget the danger of ghettoization.

References Cited

Barrett, David, ed. 1982. *World Christian Encyclopedia.* Nairobi: Oxford University Press.

Berkhof, Hendrikus. 1979. *Christian Faith: An Introduction to the Study of the Faith.* Trans. Sierd Woudstra. Grand Rapids: Eerdmans.

Farley, Wendy. 1990. *Tragic Vision and Divine Compassion: A Contemporary Theodicy.* Louisville: Westminster/John Knox Press.

Gilkey, Langdon. 1991. *Through the Tempest.* Minneapolis: Fortress Press.

Griffith-Jones, E. 1926. *The Dominion of Man.* London: Hodder & Stoughton.

Handy, Robert T. 1977. *A History of the Churches in the United States and Canada.* New York: Oxford University Press.

Jones, E. Stanley, Kenneth Scott Latourette, and John A. Mackay. 1934. *The Christian Message for Today.* New York: Round Table Press.

Kee, Howard Clark et al., eds. 1991. *Christianity: A Social and Cultural History.* New York and Toronto: Macmillan Publishing Co. and Collier Macmillan.

Küng, Hans. 1986. The Freedom of Religions, in *Attitudes Towards Other Religions,* Owen C. Thomas, ed. Lanham, Md.: University Press of America.

———. 1988. *Theology for the Third Millennium.* Trans. Peter Heinegg. New York: Doubleday Anchor Books.

Lash, Christopher. 1991. *The True and Only Heaven: Progress and Its Critics.* New York and London: W. W. Norton.

Lindbeck, George. 1984. *The Nature of Doctrine.* Philadelphia: Westminster Press.

McManners, John, ed. 1990. *The Oxford Illustrated History of Christianity.* Oxford and New York: Oxford University Press.

Mead, Sidney E. 1963. *The Lively Experiment.* New York: Harper & Row.

Roof, Wade Clark, and William McKinney. 1987. *American Mainline Religion: Its Changing Shape and Future.* New Brunswick and London: Rutgers University Press.

Taylor, John. 1990. "The Future of Christianity," in John McManners, ed., *The Oxford Illustrated History of Christianity.* Oxford and New York: Oxford University Press.

Tillich, Paul. 1952. *The Course To Be.* New Haven and London: Yale University Press.

Tracy, David. *Plurality and Ambiguity.* 1987. San Francisco: Harper & Row.

Wentz, Richard E. 1984. "The American Spirituality of Loren Eiseley." *The Christian Century.* April 25, 1984, pp. 430f.